BACCHAE

Euripides is thought to have been born around 485 BC in Attica. Along with Aeschylus and Sophocles, he is one of the three Ancient Greek tragedians whose work is still enjoyed today. His most famous works are *Medea* and the *Bacchae*. Euripides died in 406 BC.

Robin Robertson has received the E.M. Forster Award from the American Academy of Arts and Letters, the Petrarca-Preis and all three Forward Prizes. His translation of *Medea* appeared in 2008 and he has published five books of poetry, most recently *Hill of Doors* (2013).

ALSO BY ROBIN ROBERTSON

Poetry

A Painted Field

Slow Air

Swithering

The Wrecking Light

Hill of Doors

Limited Editions

Camera Obscura

Actaeon: The Early Years

Translation

The Deleted World

Medea

As Editor

32 Countries

Mortification

Love Poet, Carpenter

EURIPIDES

Bacchae

TRANSLATED AND INTRODUCED BY
Robin Robertson

VINTAGE

1 3 5 7 9 10 8 6 4 2

Vintage
20 Vauxhall Bridge Road,
London SW1V 2SA

Vintage Classics is part of the Penguin Random House
group of companies whose addresses can be found at
global.penguinrandomhouse.com

Penguin
Random House
UK

Copyright © Robin Robertson 2014

Robin Robertson has asserted his right to be identified
as the author of this Work in accordance with the Copyright,
Designs and Patents Act 1988

First published in Great Britain by Vintage in 2014

www.vintage-books.co.uk

A CIP catalogue record for this book is available
from the British Library

ISBN 9780099577386

Printed and bound by Clays Ltd, St Ives plc

Penguin Random House is committed to a sustainable future
for our business, our readers and our planet. This book is made
from Forest Stewardship Council® certified paper.

MIX
Paper from
responsible sources
FSC
www.fsc.org FSC® C018179

for James Lasdun

We turn to the gods
but the gods turn us;
we turn to the gods
and are torn apart.

CONTENTS

INTRODUCTION

EURIPIDES

We know next to nothing about Euripides: an approximate date of birth – 485–480 BC – and a probable date of death – 407 or 406 BC. It is thought he was born on the island of Salamis, west of Athens, that he spent most of his life in the township of Phyla, north of Mt Hymettus, near the capital, and that he died in Macedonia.

The one accurate ancient source we have is the *Didaskalia*: a compilation of Aristotle's lists of the plays produced at the Dionysian festival in Athens. This provides the names of the dramatists, the plays, the principal actors and the prizes awarded. Euripides is recorded as the author of ninety-two plays (of which only nineteen survive), but he won the first prize only four times, and once posthumously for the *Bacchae*. Whether this was due to the high quality of the contemporary competition or Athenian hostility to his work is hard to say.

The life of Euripides coincided with the great period of Athenian culture when the empire was consolidated and the city was established as the cultural hub of the Greek-speaking world. Beginning with the Greek victories over the invading Persians at Marathon (490 BC) and Salamis (480 BC), this fertile half-century ended with the outbreak of the Peloponnesian War in 431 BC, the year his *Medea* was first performed. This war between Athens and Sparta lasted twenty-seven years and ended in Athenian defeat in 404 BC. At some time between the catastrophic naval campaign in Sicily (415–413 BC) and the end of the war, Euripides left Athens for voluntary exile in Macedonia. Tradition has it that he met a grotesquely violent end: torn apart either by dogs – like Actaeon – or by women – like Pentheus. Three new plays were found after his death: the *Bacchae*, *Iphigenia at Aulis* and a third tragedy, which has subsequently disappeared. All three were staged at the Great Dionysia, probably in 405 BC.

GREEK TRAGEDY

In the fifth century BC, epic poetry was the conventional art form and tragedy was a relatively recent Athenian invention, originating – according to Aristotle – in the dithyrambs: choral songs in honour of Dionysus. The three great exponents of the new form were Aeschylus, Sophocles and Euripides, and they quickly established the ground rules: a mythological subject matter that used the tight focus of the family (and its associated duties and transgressions, loves and loathings) to develop wider civic implications in the state – while still allowing the drama to fall, in the end, under the inevitable sway of the gods.

STAGING

The *Bacchae* was first performed in the huge open-air theatre of Dionysus on the south slope of the Athenian acropolis, as part of the Great Dionysia – a competitive drama festival held every spring, in honour of the god, before an audience of between 15,000 and 20,000 people, predominantly male, sitting in the semi-circular rows of stepped seats in the *theatron*. There was a raised wooden stage, at the back of which was a single-storey stage-building, a *skênê*, which represented a house, temple or palace, with a large circular area below, known as the *orchêstra*, where the Chorus sang and danced. There were three points of entry to the acting area: from the *skênê*, and from two entrances – or *eisodoi* – to the right and left of the stage. The dramatists also had two mechanical features at their disposal: the *ekkyklêma*, a wheeled platform on which a tableau of actors could be grouped, and the *mêchanê*, a crane on which a god could arrive or depart.

There were usually three speaking actors, who were all male, and masked, the masks allowing them to assume different characters. The Chorus, made up of twelve to fifteen male performers, had an importance in Greek tragedy that is now largely lost to us. The Chorus had a central role: their dancing and their sung choral odes provided not just a counterpoint to the drama, but some of the finest lyric poetry. They generally represented the decent objective view: fellow citizens and interested spectators, offering an ethical and religious commentary on the action of the play. We find their relatives in Shakespeare, in moral touchstones such as Enobarbus in *Antony and Cleopatra* or Kent in *King Lear*. In the *Bacchae*, however, the Chorus is specified as 'Asian Bacchae' and they take an unusually partisan position, with their odes commenting more directly on events than previously. Almost all the dramatic action takes place offstage and is reported by an eyewitness or messenger, and is then reflected on by the Chorus.

THE BACKGROUND

The theatre audiences of Athens were highly sophisticated, and would have come to these plays with a full grounding in the great corpus of Greek myths. The word *mythos* means, literally, 'story', and these stories were regarded as morality tales of the ancestors. As contemporary readers are now increasingly unfamiliar with classical mythology, and therefore the background to the play and its characters – the story of Cadmus building Thebes and his disastrous dynasty; the character of Tiresias, the blind seer; the miraculous birth of Dionysus, the death of his mother and his revenge on Thebes – it is worth rehearsing those stories here.

Thebes, Cadmus and Harmonia

Cadmus was the son of the Phoenician king Agenor and his wife Telephassa, and brother of Europa. When Zeus took the form of a bull and abducted Europa, Agenor sent his three sons in different directions to try and find her. Eventually, the Delphic Oracle told Cadmus to abandon the hunt for his sister and instead follow a cow with a white mark like a full moon on both her sides. Where she lay down to rest he must build a city.

The cow took Cadmus to a place in Boeotia, and Cadmus decided to sacrifice her to Athene. He sent some of his men to fetch water from a nearby spring, not realising it was guarded by a dragon, said to be an offspring of Ares. When they did not return, Cadmus went to the spring, only to find them being devoured. After a long fight, the dragon was killed and, on Athene's instructions, Cadmus sowed half its teeth in the ground. Immediately, armed men sprang from the earth. Cadmus threw a stone into their midst and, each thinking he was being attacked by the others, they fought among themselves until only five were left standing. These warriors, the Spartoi ('Sown Men'), were the ancestors of the noble families of Thebes.

As a punishment for killing the dragon, Cadmus spent eight years in the service of the god Ares. At the end of this time he was granted the hand of Harmonia, the daughter of Ares and Aphrodite. Cadmus then founded his city and called it Cadmeia, later renaming it Thebes, and was assisted by Echion, one of the Spartoi, who subsequently married one of Cadmus's daughters, Agave. Cadmus would later cede his kingdom to Agave's son, Pentheus.

The dynasty of Cadmus and Harmonia was doomed. Their four daughters – Ino, Agave, Autonoe and Semele – were persecuted by Hera, the vindictive wife of Zeus. Agave would become the mother of Pentheus, the ill-fated king; Autonoe's only son would be the hunter, Actaeon, who chanced upon the goddess Artemis bathing and was punished by being transformed into a stag, and who was then torn apart by his own hounds. In some stories, Ino was driven mad and killed herself; in others she survives to join her sisters, Agave and Autonoe, in the Dionysian rites on Mt Cithaeron which form the bloody focus of the *Bacchae*. The fourth daughter, Semele, does not appear in the drama as she has already been killed, while carrying Zeus's son (and the central figure of this play) Dionysus.

Tiresias

The companion to the aged Cadmus in the *Bacchae* is the equally elderly Tiresias, the renowned blind soothsayer. Always accurate in his prophecies but famously reluctant to deliver them, Tiresias played a pivotal role in the story of Oedipus – resisting the king's request for the name of the killer of Laius, his father, before being forced to reveal that it was Oedipus himself who had committed the crime. (Oedipus, it's worth remembering, has a link with the *Bacchae's* killing ground, Mt Cithaeron: his parents left him there to die, as a newborn child, and years later he wandered the same slopes: old, self-blinded and mad with grief.) Tiresias later featured in the *Odyssey* and was one of Eliot's personae in *The Waste Land*.

Tiresias's unorthodox sexual past began on a walk, when he came upon a pair of coupling snakes, which he struck with his stick. Hera punished Tiresias by transforming him into a woman. After seven years, Tiresias was out walking and again found snakes copulating; he immediately set about them with his stick in the hope that the charm would be reversed – which it was.

Some years later, Zeus and Hera were arguing about who got more pleasure from sex: men or women. To settle the argument, they called for Tiresias, who had lived as both. Tiresias took the side of Zeus, saying that women's pleasure was greater, and Hera, in her fury, turned him blind. As no god can undo the actions of another, Zeus balanced the loss of light with a prize, giving Tiresias long life and knowledge of the future: the double-edged gift of second sight.

Dionysus

Dionysus was the product of the union, in Thebes, between Zeus and the mortal, Semele, and his birth was most unusual. When Hera heard that Zeus's seduction of Semele had resulted in pregnancy she decided to destroy her rival. Hera went to the girl disguised as her nurse and made her doubt that her lover had really been the king of the gods. She advised Semele to settle her mind by making Zeus appear before her in his full glory. Bound by an oath to grant Semele any wish, he did so, coming to her as the great storm-god, and she was consumed by the fire of his lightning bolts. As she was dying, Zeus snatched the unborn child from the ashes and stitched it into his thigh – where it could grow until it was ready to be born full-term. As a result, Dionysus is often known by the epithet 'twice-born' and is unique in having two mothers: one female, one male.

After his birth, Hermes took the child to the nymphs of Mt Nysa (which some say he is named after), who brought him up and protected him from the remorseless Hera. As he grew to manhood, Dionysus travelled widely in the east, through Egypt, Syria and Phrygia, dispensing wine to mortals and celebrating his rites in the company of his maenads, or Bacchae: wearing fawn-skins and ivy wreaths and carrying the holy thyrsus, a fennel rod wound with ivy and headed with a sharp pine cone.

Because of this time spent travelling, his habit of sudden appearances and departures, and his portrayal as a beardless, asexual youth, he was often thought of as a latecomer to the pantheon, or a foreign god – neither of which is the case, as his name has been found in the Linear B tablets, dating from *c.*1250 BC.

The idea of Dionysus as a stranger from unknown lands, from *elsewhere*, is a result of the god's volatility: he arrives in his own turbulence, bringing great ferment and often catastrophe, then vanishes. He is the god of epiphanies – sudden spiritual manifestations – and of transformation, and there is more shapeshifting associated with Dionysus than with any other Greek god except for his father Zeus – whose metamorphoses were usually prompted by his pursuit of women.

The most enigmatic, disruptive and unpredictable god in the Greek pantheon, Dionysus was primarily the god of wild nature, theatre, dance and wine. In him we see the vitality, instinct and implacable power that we find so admirable in the animal world. His counterpart in the Roman pantheon, Bacchus, seems, in comparison, a hopeless, one-dimensional caricature: a bloated, pleasure-seeking drunk. Dionysus brought wine to mortals, and with it all aspects of inebriation: relaxation, excitement and abandon – a forgetting of griefs – but also violence, sickness, sorrow and ruin. However, as you would expect from a god that embodies contradiction and duality, this gift of wine was a complicated one. It was a joy and a burden, but it was also the lubricant for the god's rituals and epiphanies, for the dissolution of boundaries. In the presence of this androgynous shapechanger and his wine, the distinctions between opposite identities break down: male and female, human and animal, individual and group. The resulting state is one of ecstasy – from the Greek *ekstasis* ('standing outside of oneself') – and the entering into this trance was an experience of oneness with the god and an initiation into his mysteries: a shift of perspective that was renewable, curative and transfiguring. The ecstatic possession of

Dionysian worship culminated in orgiastic mountain rites involving *sparagmos* (the tearing apart of a living creature) and *ômophagia* (the eating of its raw flesh); by devouring the flesh of the creature, which is an incarnation of the god, the celebrants partook of his divinity.

With these attributes of ambiguity, risk and amorality, Dionysus feels strikingly modern. A *noir* god, he is the detached, disaffected, protean stranger that slips from the shadows: a barely contained power, moving from one identity to another, from this world to the next. He cannot be defined, placed or even precisely named. As he transcends all forms and evades all categories he takes on the aspect of the Other. He is the only god that dies, but as the god of nature and vegetation he dies and is then reborn – prompting some commentators to remark on parallels with the Christian myth: both are sons of a mortal mother and the divine ruler of the world, both appear on Earth in human form, both are killed and resurrected. Dionysus – for all his destructive power and volatility – is playful, ironic, liberated and imaginative; he is the Greek god most like us: the closest, you could say, to being 'human'.

THE PLAY

The *Bacchae* continues to escape any critical consensus because its subject – among other things – is the irrational, and how conventional intellectual resources wither in the face of a wildness, a potency beyond reason. Appropriately for a play about Dionysus, the most elusive of all gods, the *Bacchae* resolutely resists any single interpretation and this, perhaps, is one of the reasons we regard it as an enduring masterpiece of drama.

The principal axis of the play is the protracted contest between the two young cousins, Pentheus and Dionysus: one human, one a god. However, neither represents, simply and consistently, one dramatic position. At first sight, Pentheus is rigid, tyrannical and self-absorbed, but he could also be seen as a brave defender of civic values. Dionysus is presented as an outsider, a religious fanatic, a fraud, or the earthly manifestation of a new and powerful religion. They have three encounters: the king questioning the stranger, Dionysus suggesting Pentheus goes to Mt Cithaeron, and the king going mad and being dressed for sacrifice. In each we see the power dynamic reversed: from Dionysus the effeminate outsider we go to Pentheus cross-dressing; the gaoler becomes the prisoner; the hunter, the quarry. And all the time, Dionysus is in charge. We see the range of his energies, effortless and mobile, increasing throughout the play.

Unknowable, untameable and metamorphic, Dionysus's nature changes under the dramatic pressure of the action, which he himself is directing. He begins as the sympathetic, wronged and almost-human deity, but as the play develops his power is channelled and tightened. He can take on any form he likes, but even as he toys with Pentheus we are increasingly aware of the tension and torque that propels the play and will deliver up the transformed, pitiless god that stalks through the final scene. The process of the play shows him turning from a mysterious, feline, softly spoken outsider, playfully bantering with the king, to a traditional Olympian deity – Homeric and anthropomorphic – before finally realising his purest form as a chaotic, eruptive life force: a raw, amoral energy. These are all Dionysus: young, and yet immortal; male, yet feminine; smiling, but savage; Theban by birth, but seen as a barbarian. Both animal and god, he spends most of the play pretending to be human, but we soon realise that he is something extraordinary: a god *in flux*.

Pentheus, on the other hand, appears hot-headed, weak and rather immature. His paranoid response to difficulty is to threaten violence or imprisonment, and his understanding of the world is crude and inaccurate: he equates the new with the subversive and 'ecstasy' with 'drunkenness' and 'carnality'. His adolescent preoccupation with sex is evident in his vaguely homoerotic interest in the stranger, in his fascination at being dressed up, and in his prurient and fatal voyeurism, during all of which he maintains close emotional ties to his mother. The way he swings from one extreme position to another (including the dramatic shift from aggressive masculinity to the passively feminine) suggests that he has not yet made a successful transition into manhood, and this would have been confirmed to the Greek audience by the robing (or 'cross-dressing') scene. Here he has failed two rites of passage – from boy to man, and from male to female – and must therefore become a sacrificial victim. Not for nothing is he named Pentheus; *penthos* being Greek for 'grief'.

The Greeks had a comprehensive and highly developed system of polarities, and they would have recognised how these underpin the text of the *Bacchae*: Greek v. foreigner, men v. women, gods v. mortals, irrational v. rational, natural abandon v. civilised order. They would have been sensitive to the textual parallels: the early scene of Tiresias summoning the costumed

Cadmus out of the house is mirrored by Dionysus calling out Pentheus dressed as a Bacchante; Pentheus remarking on the stranger's feminine attributes, only to put on later the clothes of a woman; threatening Dionysus with stoning and decapitation, only to suffer these fates himself; wanting to see the Bacchae, which he does – 'but not as well as they saw him' (1075). The Greeks would have understood how the gender reversals, along with Pentheus's longing to be back in his mother's arms (965–70), indicated a passivity and a failure to mature successfully. For the audience in Athens, the emphasis on these parallels, reversals and oppositions highlights one of the central moral messages of the play: the importance of achieving equilibrium in life.

The crucial power balance in the play is between the rational and the irrational, as represented by Pentheus and Dionysus, and this conflict can be identified in the clash between restraint and release, sanity and madness, and the human and the animal. In *The Birth of Tragedy*, Nietzsche distinguishes between the two oppositional human artistic impulses, Apollonian and Dionysian. The first was solid, ordered, restrained and learned, while the second was fluid, chaotic, excessive and primal. The Dionysian tendency was to break down boundaries – both social and personal – effacing the individual in a coalescence with nature, assisted by the harmonising power of wine and dance; the Apollonian tendency offered a composed critical and ethical distance. Nietzsche argued that the ideal creative state was an equilibrium between the two aspects.

Tiresias points out that extreme Apollonian rigidity of thought is a dangerous kind of madness (310–27) and we see sanity and derangement inverted later in the play when Pentheus appears for the decisive robing scene, dressed as a Bacchante, saying:

> I see two suns in the sky;
> two cities of Thebes, each with seven gates.
> And you, my guide, you seem to be a bull.
> Horns grow from your head.
> Were you a beast all along? For you are a bull now.
>
> (918–22)

Seeing two suns is a traditional sign of madness, but Pentheus is also experiencing Dionysus in his epiphanic animal form as a horned bull. The king encountered the bull-god before, when he was trying to tie up the stranger (617), but this is different. In this pivotal scene, with its remarkable blend of the comic and tragic, we watch a caricature of the ritual process of trance and transformation, in which the sane king is now mad and dressed in women's clothes, and where Dionysus, who was pretending to be a man, has now taken the form of a bull, the true incarnation of the god. They are on the threshold of the Dionysian world, which – as we have seen before, and will see again shortly – can be a place of carnage. It's important to recall, though, the beautiful lyric passages from the Chorus – particularly in lines 864–78 – that provide a real sense of that world's pastoral serenity: the followers of the god living soberly at one with nature, blessed with the god's abundance. These vivid portrayals of the benevolence of ecstatic religion are corroborated and reinforced by the reports of the king's messenger and so offer an important corrective; the Dionysian world is a kind of paradise for the celebrants, but when the privacy of the sacred mysteries is breached, by hunters or voyeurs or god-deniers, the idyll becomes an abattoir.

This robing scene (where the god is costume designer, stylist and choreographer) is a darkly comic charade – the most obvious of a number of plays within the play – and the *Bacchae* is, after all, a play *about* Dionysus, performed in the theatre *of* Dionysus and written, directed, stage-managed and acted *by* Dionysus, with a narrative created to expose Pentheus and punish Thebes. The play is a metadrama – a drama about drama – that uses transformation, via illusion or disguise, to undermine conventional distinctions between true and false, the real and the unreal. Tiresias and Cadmus appear in ivy and fawn-skins – shrewd, pragmatic sophists dressed as Bacchantes out of expediency; Pentheus is given the same disguise for different reasons, then enacts a parody of a sacred rite; Dionysus assumes human form for much of the play, but is always shimmering towards metamorphosis, particularly the bestial, and is identified in the play with the bull, the snake, the lion and, through his maenads, the deer.

Once Pentheus has departed for the mountain, the farce is over and the play starts to spiral to its horrific conclusion. The king has brought death on himself: in his vanity and blindness he has denied the god and his punishment for this transgression will be an inversion of the ritual mysteries he is so keen to spy on. He has been dressed in women's clothes, a human turned briefly into a sacrificial beast, and will now be hunted. The manner of his death has already been foreshadowed by that of Actaeon – cousin to both Pentheus and Dionysus – but it will not be his own dogs that tear him apart, it will be his mother and his aunts, and Agave will boast of her kill.

The tragedy of the play is largely invested in the character of Agave. Onstage for one scene only – probably the finest recognition scene in tragedy – her role is to come to her senses and realise what she has done, then to pass into the most acute suffering, allowing the play a moral grandeur and dignity. As she grieves, the loyalties of both the audience and the partisan Chorus move irrevocably from Dionysus to Agave. The god's final, heartless ferocity is balanced against the devastating anguish of a mother who has unwittingly murdered her son. The pity and compassion we feel for Agave, and for her father Cadmus, tip the play's emotional balance from the charismatic god to the broken mortals – and towards a victory for humanity.

Not until the very end of the play does the ground stop shifting, and the illusions fall away. Only when Dionysus has finished playing with the human world, delivered his *coup de grâce* and left, only then can we see clearly and assess the damage. What we understand is that society must allow room for the irrational, in healthy balance with the rational. What we see is Agave trying to piece together the body parts of the son she has dismembered. What we feel is predominantly human pity, but also the distinct aftershocks of being in the presence of this exquisite, complex, catastrophic god.

NOTE ON THE TEXT

There are no manuscripts in the hand of Euripides or, indeed, any of the classical authors: the only transcription of the *Bacchae* that survives is from the fourteenth century, and it is a copy of a copy. Over the centuries there have been ample opportunities for textual corruption, and texts of the play more academic than this one offer solutions of reconstruction 'by conjecture'. They also address the problem of interpolation, where new matter appears to have been added to expand or elaborate the original.

In the *Bacchae* there is the additional problem of lacunae in the text at lines 1300 and 1329, which have been the topic of some debate. Rather than introduce speculative connective tissue I have indicated briefly, in footnotes, the likely substance of the lost material. At line 1301, where Agave asks Cadmus about her son's corpse, saying 'Is he complete, and decently arranged?', the missing response would be something like: 'All his parts are laid out here, all but the head.' Agave could then place the head of Pentheus with his other remains. The gap in the text at line 1329 seems more substantial and problematic. Agave says to Cadmus, 'Father, you see how changed my fortunes are . . .' It is likely that Agave would then piece together the body parts of her son, mourning each one individually. The text begins again with Dionysus – no longer incognito, but revealed as a god – giving a detailed account of what the future holds for Cadmus. It seems plausible that the missing textual matter might include the god's revelations about the fates of the other characters – preceded, perhaps, with a reasoned explanation for his terrible retribution.

I have used the Loeb Classical Library edition, edited and translated by David Kovacs, as my primary source, and have consulted a number of fine English translations – including those by William Arrowsmith, John Davie, James Morwood and J. Michael Walton. As with my recent edition of *Medea*, my main concern has been to provide a text that can be read – and acted – easily: an English version that is as true to the Greek of two and a half thousand years ago as it is to the way English is spoken now.

The line numbers in this edition refer to the Greek text.

ACKNOWLEDGEMENTS

This translation was made in Marfa, Texas; my thanks go to Jo Chapman, Martha Jessup and Patrick Lannan of the Lannan Foundation for their hospitality. I am also grateful to my colleagues in Vintage: Rachel Cugnoni and, particularly, Laura Hassan.

BACCHAE

BACCHAE

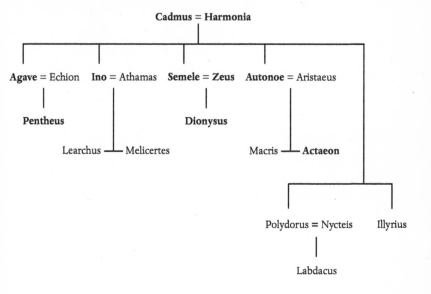

CHARACTERS

DIONYSUS, *the god, also known as Bacchus,*
Bromius, Evius, Iacchus, the Roaring One
CHORUS *of Asian Bacchae*
TIRESIAS, *blind Theban prophet*
CADMUS, *grandfather of Pentheus*
PENTHEUS, *king of Thebes*
SERVANT *of Pentheus*
MESSENGER, *a herdsman*
SECOND MESSENGER, *Pentheus's attendant*
AGAVE, *mother of Pentheus*

Outside the royal palace of Thebes.

Enter Dionysus.

DIONYSUS

I am the god, Dionysus. Dionysus, son of Zeus.
I have taken human form and come back here, to Thebes.
Semele, daughter of Cadmus, gave birth to me here,
midwifed by the lightning fire.
Over there are the waters of Dirce and Ismenus;
and there, by the palace, the tomb of my mother
and the shell of her house, smouldering
with the living flame of Zeus.
Hera's jealous hatred burns here still.
Cadmus, my grandfather,
held these ruins sacred to his daughter;   10
I honour him for that.
It was I who made these vines grow here:
so green around this grave, this shrine.

Far behind me lie golden Lydia, and Phrygia
from where I came,
making my way through the sun-lands of Persia,

7

the forts of Bactria, the wastes of the Medes –
I passed through rich Arabia, and those parts of Asia
where Greeks and outlanders live side by side
in towered cities by the sea.
There I established my rites and mysteries,
revealed myself as a god. I set all Asia dancing,
and now I have come to Greece.
Returned to the place of my first birth:
come back, here, to Thebes.

This city is the first in Greece to ring with my ecstasies, 20
with the cries of women, clothed in fawn-skin,
holding the thyrsus – my sacred spear, bound in ivy.
But why here? Why Thebes?
Because my mother's sisters
– who should have been the last to start such rumours –
claimed that I was *not* the son of Zeus,
that Semele's lover was mortal,
that my god-like birth was a trick   30
thought up by Cadmus to save his daughter's name.
That Zeus had killed my mother with his lightning bolt
deliberately, for her false claim that they were lovers.
And so, in return, I have made them mad:
stung them from their homes and up into the mountains,
out of their minds. And all the rest,
all the women of Thebes, are with those
daughters of Cadmus now – and all of them
dressed in the trappings of my sacred rites.
Driven, delirious, out of their houses,

they huddle on the cliffs under the pines.
Thebes must learn its lesson, like it or not,
that it needs initiation in my mysteries.   40
It will see my mother's innocence
when it sees me as a god; as the son of a god.

Cadmus is old now,
and has passed his throne to Pentheus –
son of Agave, another of his daughters.
And young Pentheus denies me: offers no libations,
makes no mention of me in prayer.
So I must teach this Pentheus, teach all of Thebes,
what kind of god I am.
Once I am established here
I will move on to other lands and show myself there.   50
But if Thebes tries to drive my Bacchae
from the mountains by force of arms,
I will marshal my Maenads and bring on war.
I have readied myself for battle:
put my deity aside and taken human form.

He calls to the Chorus.

So, my women, my loyal band of worshippers
who followed me from Mount Tmolus,
from Lydia and the outer lands: come!
Bring the drums we brought from Phrygia
– Mother Rhea's drums and mine –   60
and beat them at the palace doors of Pentheus!

Let the citizens of Thebes take notice.
Let them see. I go now to Mount Cithaeron,
to the Bacchae, to join them in their dance.

Enter Chorus. Exit Dionysus.

CHORUS
    Out from Asia, down from sacred Tmolus we have come,
    in the sweet service of Bromius
    – work that brings a happy weariness –
    crying out for him, Bacchus, Dionysus!
    You on the street! You on the road! You in the palace!
    Come out, and hold your tongues in piety.   70
    For we shall sing the ancient hymn of Dionysus.

    Blessèd are those who know the mysteries of the god.
    Blessèd are those who consecrate their lives to worship.
    Blessèd are those who give themselves up to the dance,
    to the mysteries, to purification on the holy mountain
    where the dance and the mysteries take place.
    Blessèd are those who observe the rites of Cybele,
    our great mother. Blessèd are those
    who wield the thyrsus, the wand of god,   80
    that wear his crown of ivy.
    On, Bacchae! On, you Bacchae!
    Bring the roaring god, the son of a god,
    from Phrygia to these streets of Greece,
    bring lord Dionysus!

He was born as his mother died under the fire of Zeus,   90
as the god's thunder broke her into flame.
Shipped by grief, the god retrieved his half-formed child
from the carnage and let it grow its last three months
sewn into his thigh, fixed by golden clasps,
hidden from his jealous wife.
Then, when the Fates brought him to term,   100
Zeus gave birth to his son –
a father, and now a kind of second mother.
Our lord, Dionysus: not just a twice-born child,
but a horned god, crowned with a wreath of serpents.
His Maenads honour him to this day
by weaving snakes into their hair.

Thebes, that nurtured Semele,
take on the garlands of ivy!
Dress yourself in green, in bryony's red berries,
in sprays of the Bacchae's oak and fir,   110
and deck your dappled fawn-skin
with twists of the whitest wool!
Take up, with care, the deadly thyrsus spear
and free the dance! The whole *land* will dance,
when Bromius leads you to the mountains
to join the waiting women –
driven from their shuttles and looms,
freed from themselves, possessed by Dionysus!

And we praise the secret chambers of the Curetes,   120
in Crete, where Zeus was born,

where they made the drum of tightened hide,
and through its heart-beat and their fierce, ecstatic dance,
they threaded the sweet breath of the Phrygian flute;
they gave the drum to Mother Rhea to beat time,
to mark the measure of the dance.
The Satyrs took it then and brought it to their festivals,   130
for the pleasure of Dionysus.

What beauty is in the mountains
when he wheels away from the pack,
fawn-skin streaming behind him, and he falls
on the goat, on the raw feast,
the smoking meal of flesh and blood.
He runs wild on the mountains of Phrygia and Lydia,   140
our leader, Bromius! *Evohé!*
The earth flows beneath him: the ground coursing
with milk and wine and the nectar of bees.
His pine torch trailing long flames
and smoke as sweet as Syrian frankincense,
he's running, dancing, hair wild behind him,   150
spurring on stragglers, rousing them all with rapturous cries,
calling: On, Bacchae! On, you Bacchae!
Glory of golden Tmolus, sing your praise to Dionysus
to the sound of the drums,
cry *Evohé!* to the Evian god, to the skirl of the pipes,   160
to lead us with our holy songs up high to the mountain,
to the mountain! And so, like a filly at her mother's side,

the Bacchante slips and jinks away,
frisking, field over field, in flight.

Enter Tiresias, old and blind, and dressed as a Bacchant.

TIRESIAS

Gatekeeper! Are you there?
Call Cadmus out of the house: Agenor's son,   170
who left Sidon to build the walls and towers of Thebes.
Tell him Tiresias is here.
He'll remember the pact we made –
one old man with another older still –
to bind the thyrsus, dress in fawn-skin
and wreathe our heads in ivy.

Enter Cadmus, similarly dressed.

CADMUS

I thought it must be you, dear friend!
I recognised your voice from inside:
wise words from a wise man.
Here I am: all ready. All dressed up in the god's outfit. 180
The god who's revealed himself to mortals.
He's my daughter's son, after all,
so we must praise him all we can.
Where should we do our dancing, do you think?
And how exactly should we dance?
We can shake these old white heads, I suppose.

You'd better lead, Tiresias: you're the wise one.
But I'm raring to go! I'll be at it day and night,
beating the ground with my stick!
How wonderful, to forget our age!

TIRESIAS

I feel just the same!
Extraordinary! I feel young enough to dance!   190

CADMUS

Shall we take a chariot up the mountain?

TIRESIAS

No, I think we should walk. It shows respect.

CADMUS

Very well. One old man leading another like a child.

TIRESIAS

The god will bring us there, effortlessly.

CADMUS

Are we the only men who'll dance for Dionysus?

TIRESIAS

The rest are blind. Only we can see.

CADMUS

We may as well get started, then. Take my hand.

TIRESIAS

Where are you? Ah. Now hold tight.

CADMUS

I am a mortal; I would never scorn a god, you know.

TIRESIAS

Wise not to trifle with divinity,   200
or with the wisdom of our fathers.
Both are beyond sophistry. People might say:
'Look at that old fool,
dancing around with ivy in his hair!'
But for the god, it is only the dance that matters.
Whatever age we are –
as long as we raise our hands to him.

CADMUS

Because you cannot see, Tiresias,   210
let me interpret for you just this once.
Young Pentheus approaches us, at speed.
The grandson to whom I handed my throne.
He seems upset. Let's hear what he has to say.

Enter Pentheus, accompanied by attendants.

PENTHEUS

I was out of the country for a few days
and I come back to *this*.

Women have deserted their homes for these
fraudulent rites – up in the woods and mountains,
dancing to celebrate some new god –
Dionysus, whoever he is.   220
Drink is at the bottom of it all.
Huge bowls stand in their midst, I'm told,
brimming with wine, and one by one the women
slip into the shadows to satisfy the lusts of men.
They say they are priestesses, sworn to Bacchus,
but it's clearly Aphrodite they adore.
I've had some of them trapped, and shackled in the prison.
The rest are still out there on the mountain –
even my mother is among them,
she who bore me to Echion,
with her sisters Ino and Autonoe, mother of Actaeon.   230
I'll hunt them down with nets.
I'll put an end to their filthy orgies.

They say some foreigner has arrived from Lydia:
one of those charlatan magicians
with blond hair that reeks of scent,
the flush of wine in his cheeks
and all the tricks of Aphrodite in his eyes.
Day and night he's with the women,
showing them his mysteries –
holding up his secret, for them to adore.

Once I catch him there'll be none of that tossing of locks   240
and waving of wands:
I'll take that head from off his body!
This is the man who claims Dionysus is a god,
that he was sewn into the thigh of Zeus!
In point of fact, he and his mother were both consumed
by lightning fire – for her lie that she had lain with Zeus.
Whoever he is, this stranger,
such insults and insolence demand nothing less than death.

He notices Cadmus and Tiresias.

And here's another miracle! The prophet Tiresias
all got up in fawn-skin, and my mother's father
dressed up as a Bacchant with a wand.   250
You look ridiculous, both of you: have you lost your wits?
I'm ashamed of you, Grandfather.
Shake off that ivy and drop that bloody stick!
This is your doing, Tiresias, I can tell:
another imported god, another chance
to make money on the side from burnt offerings
and reading auguries from the guts of birds.
If you weren't so ancient
I'd have you locked up with those Bacchic women
for bringing this wickedness, this madness to Thebes.   260
It's always the same: as soon as you allow drink
and women at a festival, everything gets sordid.

CHORUS LEADER

This is blasphemy!
Stranger, have you no respect for the gods –
or for Cadmus who sowed the dragon's teeth
to bring forth men from the earth?
Will you disgrace Echion, one of those men,
and defame your own house?

TIRESIAS

When a wise man has an honest case to plead, then
eloquence, I find, is very easy to achieve.
You think yourself clever, and have a smooth tongue,
but your words are foolish.
The man whose power lies in his conceit   270
does not make a good citizen.

The new god you ridicule will be a great power in Greece.
Let me explain, young man, the two blessings of human life.
Firstly Demeter, Mother Earth – call her what you will –
sustains us mortals with the gift of grain, of solid food.
But he who came next – son of Semele –
matched her gift to man: he brought us wine.
And wine brought peace to the troubled mind,   280
gave an end to grief, and gave us sleep – blessèd sleep –
a forgetting of our sadnesses.
He, a god himself, is poured out in honour of the gods.
Through that holy wine we win their favour.

And you sneer at that story
that he was sewn into the thigh of Zeus.
Shall I teach you what that really means?
When Zeus snatched his son from the flames
of the thunderbolt and brought him to Olympus,
Hera wanted to cast the child from heaven.   290
Zeus fooled his wife by breaking off a piece of the sky
and fashioning it to the shape and size of Dionysus.
He showed her the manikin and handed it over.
As time passed, men confused the words of the story.
Instead of saying 'Zeus showed her the sky'
it was garbled over the years to 'sewed in the thigh'.
And so, a myth is made.

And this god is a prophet, too.
The power of ecstasy brings the power of second sight.
When the god enters someone in full force   300
he gives them an eye into the future.
You can also find this god in the field of war, alongside Ares.
An army is drawn up for battle,
but before a spear is lifted
a panic seizes them and they run.
This panic comes from Dionysus.

One day you will see him bounding on the cliffs of Delphi,
dancing with pine torches between the double peaks,
hair ablaze, his wand in the air: his power great in Greece.
Listen to me, young Pentheus.   310
Brute force does not make a man strong.

And sickness of the mind is never wisdom.
Receive the god into your kingdom,
pour libations, cover your head with ivy, join the dance!

As for the women, it is not for the god to enforce chastity.
Dionysus releases their true nature. Even plunged in delirium,
a virtuous soul does not turn vile.

Don't you understand?
You know yourself what a thrill it is
to stand at your gates and hear the city cry out 'Pentheus!' 320
Well, Dionysus, too, delights in glory. Give him his due.
I and Cadmus, whom you also ridicule,
have wreathed our grey heads in ivy and will dance.
Your words will not persuade me to fight against a god.
It is you who are mad, grievously mad.
You are drugged with madness, which no drug can cure.

CHORUS LEADER
Wise words, old man. Apollo would approve
the honour that you do to the great god Bromius.

CADMUS
My boy, Tiresias gives you good advice.   330
Your home is here with us, with our customs and traditions,
not outside, on your own. You are distracted, I know,
but your cleverness means nothing now.

Even if, as you insist, this god is *not* a god,
it does no harm to say he is.
A white lie, with some benefit besides:
Semele will be seen as the mother of a god,
and honour comes to the family.
Remember what happened to your cousin, Actaeon?
Torn to pieces and devoured by his own hounds
because he bragged that his prowess at hunting   340
surpassed the skills of Artemis.
Don't let his fate be yours.

He moves towards Pentheus.

Come, let me crown you with ivy.
Join in giving honour to the god.

PENTHEUS

Take your hands away! Go and play your dancing games,
but don't smear your madness over me.

He turns to Tiresias.

I'll make him pay,
this man who brought my father down to this.

To his attendants.

Go, someone, quickly,
to where this so-called prophet reads his auguries,
find his *sanctum sanctorum*, and turn it over.
Prise it up with levers, raze it to the ground.
Throw his garlands and headgear to the winds: 350
that will hurt him most of all!

Exit servant.

The rest of you: search the city
and find that effeminate stranger,
the one who's polluting our women, emptying our beds.
When you catch him, bring him here in chains
so he can die as he deserves – by stoning.
We will see how he dances then.

Exit other servants.

TIRESIAS

Poor young fool:
you have no idea what you're saying.
You were raving before,
but now I think you may have gone insane.
Come, Cadmus, let us go and pray for this lunatic 360
and for our city; pray the god does not
fork down vengeance.
Come, take your thyrsus
and we'll help each other on the road.
It would be too shameful – wouldn't it –

two old men stumbling and falling in a heap?
Still, we must go regardless:
we owe it to Dionysus, son of Zeus.
I only hope that Pentheus does not bring his sorrow
down upon your house.
His foolish words will end in folly –
and this is not some prophecy, Cadmus: this is fact.

Exit Cadmus and Tiresias.

CHORUS

Do you hear him, sacred queen of heaven,   370
who soars above us on your golden wings?
Do you hear the slights of Pentheus,
his blasphemies against the son of Semele,
god of garlands and feasts –
Bromius, the Roaring One?
Dionysus, who has given us so much:
uniting us in dance,
to the sound of the flute and our own delight,   380
loosening all our cares
with the wine-bowls' warm red gleam,
until the revellers dip their ivy crowns
and are carried into sleep.

Unbridled tongues or actions bring disaster;
tranquillity and common sense
will keep the house together.   390
The gods gaze down on us

from their huge height
and know that cleverness is not wisdom,
that over-reaching mortals
simply shorten their lives.
Life is brief enough as it is,
so hold it all to hand.
Wild ambition is a kind of madness:
stretch too hard for the summit   400
and you will fail and fall
and plummet back to land.

Let me go to Cyprus, island of Aphrodite,
home of those who cast the spells of love!
To rainless Paphos,
greened by a hundred streams!
To fair Pieria, home of the Muses,   410
on the slopes of Mount Olympus!
Take me there, Lord Dionysus,
to the haunts of Desire and the three Graces;
take me where we can dance,
and celebrate you, and worship as we please.

The god, the son of Zeus,
delights in feasts and festivals,
loves the goddess Peace,
who lets boys grow into men.   420
He shares his gift of wine, of bliss,
with rich and poor,
and hates all those

who have no care for this:
who would not live
a life of blessedness, day and night.
He tells us to avoid ambition,
pride, excess, to see
what the simple man believes
and practises as good.   430
I accept this covenant,
this way of life, as true.

Enter a Servant, with others of the king's retinue, leading
Dionysus in chains.

SERVANT

We are here, my lord, with the prey you sent us after.
He is tame, though: made no attempt to run
when we reached him – never even paled.
He just stood there, smiling,
holding out his wrists for us to tie.   440
It was so easy, I felt ashamed.
'Stranger,' I said, 'I'm not to blame.
I'm taking you on the orders of Pentheus.'

By the way, those women
you had shackled and sent to the dungeon?
They're gone. Clean away.
They're bounding up the mountain now,
calling for Bromius.
The chains just fell off them, like magic,

and the doors unbolted and swung open,
all by themselves.
I tell you something,
this man who's come to Thebes is full of miracles.   450
That's all I know. The rest is up to you.

PENTHEUS

Untie his hands. We have him in our net.
He may be quick, but he won't be dancing out of this.

So. Not entirely unattractive – at least to women, I suppose,
which is why you're here in Thebes.
Such long hair.
Not a wrestler then, I take it?
So long, it frames your cheeks. And such pale skin!
You must be looking after it: staying out of the sun.
Only coming out to play at night, hunting Aphrodite.

Right then. Where are you from?

DIONYSUS

That's easy enough.   460
You've heard of Mount Tmolus and her flowers?

PENTHEUS

I know of it. It stands above Sardis.

DIONYSUS

I come from there. My country is Lydia.

PENTHEUS

Whose rituals are these you've brought to Greece?

DIONYSUS

Dionysus, son of Zeus, initiated me.

PENTHEUS

You have a Zeus in Lydia, do you, spawning new gods?

DIONYSUS

There is only one Zeus, who was Semele's lover here.

PENTHEUS

When he conscripted you, this god:
was that in a dream or face to face?

DIONYSUS

He revealed his mysteries in front of me,
as close as I am to you now.

PENTHEUS

Ah yes, the mysteries.   470
What form do they take, these mysteries of yours?

DIONYSUS

They are secrets only initiates may know.

PENTHEUS

What benefits accrue to these 'initiates'?

DIONYSUS

I am forbidden to say, but they are many.

PENTHEUS

Now you're just trying to make me curious!

DIONYSUS

The mysteries are not for the unbeliever.

PENTHEUS

You say you saw the god. What form did he assume?

DIONYSUS

Whatever form he wished. His choice.

PENTHEUS

You're evading the question. That makes no sense.

DIONYSUS

Sense is nonsense to a fool.

PENTHEUS

Is this the first place you have brought the god?   480

DIONYSUS

Outlanders dance everywhere for Dionysus.

PENTHEUS

Barbarians are far less intelligent than Greeks.

DIONYSUS

In this case *more* intelligent. Customs differ.

PENTHEUS

These mysteries. Do you practise them by day, or night?

DIONYSUS

Mostly by night. Dark is better for devotion.

PENTHEUS

Better for lechery and the taking of women.

DIONYSUS

That happens in daylight too.

PENTHEUS

You'll pay for all this sophistry.

DIONYSUS

And you, for your blasphemy.

PENTHEUS

What a bold Bacchant. You wrestle well, with words.   490

DIONYSUS

Tell me my fate. What punishment do you propose?

PENTHEUS

First I'll cut off these love-locks.

DIONYSUS

My hair is sacred. It is grown for the god.

Pentheus cuts off some of Dionysus's hair.

PENTHEUS

Now the magic wand . . . hand it over.

DIONYSUS

Take it from me yourself. It belongs to Dionysus.

Pentheus takes the thyrsus.

PENTHEUS

Then we'll put you in chains, in prison.

DIONYSUS

Dionysus will free me, whenever I wish.

PENTHEUS

Call for him all you like, you and your Bacchae.

DIONYSUS

He is here now. He sees how I am suffering.

PENTHEUS

Oh, really? I can't see him anywhere.   500

DIONYSUS

He is with me, where I am. The godless cannot see.

PENTHEUS

Seize him! He mocks me, and he mocks Thebes.

DIONYSUS

Do not try and chain me. I am sane and you are not.

PENTHEUS

Chain him! I am the power here.

DIONYSUS

You do not know what your life is,
or what you are doing, or who you are.

PENTHEUS

I am Pentheus. Son of Echion. Son of Agave.

DIONYSUS

Your very name spells 'sorrow'. It suits you well.

PENTHEUS

Take him away! Lock him in the stables;
he'll have all the dark he needs.
Let him dance there.   510
As for that pack of women,
his partners in crime,
I'll either sell them as slaves
or have them work the looms.
That will silence their damn drums.

DIONYSUS

I will go, though not to suffering, since that cannot be.
Only you will suffer: for this insolence,
punished by the very god whose existence you deny.
Put chains on me, and you are binding Dionysus.

Exit Dionysus and Pentheus with retinue.

CHORUS

Queen Dirce, sacred river,   520
child of the waters of Achelous,
I call on you:
you who once held
the son of Zeus in your currents,
after his father snatched him from the pyre

then put him in his thigh and shouted:
'You are Dithyrambus, enter this male womb.
I name you Bacchus, and proclaim to Thebes
that she should call you by that name.'
But now, blessèd Dirce, I come to your banks   530
bringing bands of worshippers
garlanded for the dance,
and you reject me.
By the clustered grapes of Dionysus,
I swear one day
you will come to know
the name of the Roaring One.

Pentheus betrays his origins:
dragon-seeded, son of Echion,   540
sprung from the earth and barely human –
like one of the Giants fighting the gods.
Pentheus threatens me
– servant of Dionysus –
with the same chains that bind my master,
cast in prison dark.
Do you see, Dionysus, son of Zeus,   550
how we are oppressed?
Come down from Olympus,
shaking your golden thyrsus,
and protect us from this tyrant!

Are you in Nysa, land of beasts?
On the ridges of Corycia?

In the glades of Olympus,
where Orpheus   560
charmed the beasts and the trees
with the playing of his lyre?
O Pieria, you are blessed!
Evius honours you,
fording the mighty Axios and the Lydias,   570
and comes through the land of horses
to dance with his Maenads! He comes!

DIONYSUS (*from within*)
Hear me! Hear me, Bacchae! I am calling!

CHORUS
Who calls? Who calls with the cry of Evius?

DIONYSUS
Hear me, Bacchae! The son of Zeus and Semele!   580

CHORUS
Bromius! Lord, come to us now! Be here!

DIONYSUS
Let the earthquake come, and shake the roots of the world!

CHORUS A
Soon the palace of Pentheus will break and fall!
Dionysus is inside! Revere him!

CHORUS B

We revere him! 590

CHORUS A

Look: the stone lintels gape from their columns!
The Roaring One is pulling down the palace from inside!

DIONYSUS

Spark the lightning bolt!
Let the flames feed on the house of Pentheus!

CHORUS

See how the palace blazes! And on the tomb of Semele,
the flame of Zeus rises and roars in reply!
Abase yourselves, Maenads: fall to your knees in awe! 600
The son of Zeus has come, pulling the house of Pentheus
down around him! Its shape held, then . . . see it –
sleeving its own fall!

The Chorus prostrate themselves. Enter Dionysus.

DIONYSUS

Women of Asia, were you so afraid you dropped to the ground?
Perhaps you saw what Dionysus did to the palace?
You must stand now, take heart, and stop shaking.

CHORUS LEADER

Light of our revels, of our world, how glad I am to see you!
Without you I was lost.

DIONYSUS

    Did you despair when I was taken away   610
    and thrown in that dungeon?

CHORUS LEADER

    What else was there left but despair?
    Who was there left to save me?
    But how did you escape from that godless man?

DIONYSUS

    I rescued myself. That part was easy.

CHORUS LEADER

    But I thought you were in chains . . .

DIONYSUS

    He thought so too. That was the start of his shaming.
    When he imagined he was binding me
    he never even touched my hands.
    I made him see what he wanted to see,
    so I had him shackle a bull instead of me.
    That took a while, I can tell you, Pentheus trying
    to throw a rope round the creature's knees and hooves.
    He was blowing hard, frustrated and furious,   620
    biting his lip and shaking off sweat.
    I sat nearby, quietly watching.

And then, Bacchus revealed himself;
he shook the palace like a toy, and sent bright tongues
of flame darting up from his mother's tomb.
Thinking his palace was ablaze,
Pentheus started running about,
shouting at servants to fetch water.
But it was all too late, of course.

Then he remembered his prisoner,
drew his sword and dashed back in.
Then Bromius made – or so it seemed to me,
I'm only guessing – he made a ghost.   630
Bursting in, Pentheus thrust and stabbed at the bright air,
thinking it was me: trying to kill the light.
Then the god finished what he'd started:
taking the palace in both hands,
he smashed it to the ground.
This is the price that Pentheus pays for trying to contain me.
I watched the sword fall through his fingers;
his shoulders sink, exhausted from the fight.
A man who dared to wage war with a god.
I left quietly and came here,
leaving that empty man behind.

But by the sound of all those heavy feet,
I think he's coming back for more.

What is there left to say? 640
But I'll be calm in the face of all his rage.
He should learn from me the ways of self-control.

Enter Pentheus with retinue.

PENTHEUS

This is maddening.
That stranger, that man I had in chains, has escaped!

What! Here he is!
How is it that you're free, standing at the gate of my palace?
Answer me!

DIONYSUS

Please calm down.

PENTHEUS

How did you escape?

DIONYSUS

Don't you remember? I said someone would set me free.

PENTHEUS

Someone? Who is this 'someone'? 650

DIONYSUS

The one who grew the clustering vine for mortals.

PENTHEUS

And made them lose their senses . . .

DIONYSUS

You insult the gift of Dionysus . . .

PENTHEUS

Bar every gate of the city!

Exit two servants.

DIONYSUS

What good will that do? What is a wall to a god?

PENTHEUS

You're clever, aren't you? But maybe not *that* clever.

DIONYSUS

I am clever enough when I need to be.

Enter a herdsman, as Messenger.

But here's a man who looks like he has something to say –
all the way from the mountains.
I'll be right here, don't worry. I won't run away.

MESSENGER

Pentheus, king of Thebes, I come from high Cithaeron, 660
where the glittering white snow still falls, on and on –

PENTHEUS

Get to the point. What is your message, messenger?

MESSENGER

Sire, I have seen the wild Bacchae,
the women who ran barefoot in frenzy from this city.
I have seen what they do: their miracles.
But . . . may I speak freely, my lord?
I fear your impatience, sire, your temper –   670

PENTHEUS

Speak. No harm will come to you, whatever you say.
Being angry with an honest man is wrong.
The more terrible the things you tell me, though,
the more terrible the punishment
for the man who brought this evil here.

MESSENGER

The sun had just risen and the earth was warming up
as we drove our herds
along the ridge to the high meadow,
when I saw three bands of women:
one led by Autonoe,   680

one by your mother, Agave, and one by Ino.
They lay exhausted,
some resting on fir branches,
others sleeping among oak leaves.
They were modest and composed, not drunk
with wine as you say,
not dancing wildly to pipe music,
or chasing Aphrodite in some ecstasy.

But then your mother must have heard the lowing   690
of our cattle and, springing to her feet, let out a cry
to stir the rest from their sleep.
And one by one they woke,
rubbing their eyes like children,
and rose – tall and straight.
What a sight it was:
old and young, some still unmarried.
What a sight.
First they stretched back to loosen their hair
and let it fall over their shoulders,
and those whose fawn-skin straps had slipped in sleep,
secured them again with snakes
that licked at their cheeks.
New mothers, who had left their babies
behind at home, drew gazelles and wolf cubs   700
to their swollen breasts
and let them feed.

They decked themselves
with crowns of ivy, oak and bryony.
One woman struck her thyrsus on a rock
and a spring of water shot out, bubbling.
Another drove her fennel wand into the ground
and the god released a jet of wine.
Those who wanted milk
simply tapped the earth
with their fingers and a fountain started.
Pure honey spurted and streamed   710
from the tips of their wands.
If you had been there, sire,
you would have gone down on your knees and prayed
to the very god you deny.

We herdsmen gathered in groups, talking and arguing
about these extraordinary things we'd seen.
Then a blow-in from the city,
who clearly had a way with words, stood up and said:
'You who live on the mountain pastures,
what say we earn ourselves the gratitude of the king   720
and hunt down Agave, Pentheus's mother,
and drag her from the dance?'
It seemed a good idea,
so we lay in ambush, camouflaged with leaves.
At the appointed time, the women came,
waving their wands for the start of the ritual,
calling on Bromius, Iacchus, son of Zeus,
till the whole mountain and its creatures

42

seemed as possessed as they were.
And then the women ran, and the world ran with them.

As it happened, Agave came
leaping towards my hiding place,
and as I stood to grab her she let out a shout: 730
'Hounds that hunt with me, we are hunted now!
Follow me! Follow me,
and use your wands as weapons against these men!'

We fled.
They would have torn us to pieces, those Bacchae.
Instead, they turned – bare-handed –
on our herd of grazing cattle.
A single woman pulled a mewling calf in two,
while others clawed apart a full-grown heifer.
There were spread ribs and broken hooves   740
flung everywhere,
and pieces of flesh hung
dripping from the trees.
Great bulls, their power and fury tightening in their horns,
lowered their heads to charge
but were wrestled to the ground
by countless female hands and flayed alive –
faster, sire, than a blink of your royal eyes.

Then they rose like birds
and swept over the plain that stretched below,
cornfields watered by the river of Asopus.   750

EURIPIDES

They swooped on Hysiae and Erythrae
on the foothills of Cithaeron, scattering everything,
turning it upside down. They snatched children
from their homes, and pillaged houses.
Everything they threw on their backs stayed there:
nothing, not even bronze or iron, fell to the earth.
Flames danced in their hair but did not burn them.
The furious villagers took up their weapons in defence
and, sire, what happened next was dreadful to see.   760
The men's spears of pointed metal drew no blood,
while the flung wands of the women ripped open flesh,
and the men turned and ran.
Women routing men! Some god was here with them.
The Bacchae then swung round and back
to where they'd started, to the green woods,
to the springs the god had made for them,
and they washed their hands of the thick blood,
while the snakes licked clean their spattered cheeks.

Whoever this god may be, sire,
I would welcome him to Thebes.
He is great in many ways – not least, I hear say,   770
for his gift of wine to mortal men.
Wine, which puts an end to sorrow and to pain.
And if there is no wine, there is no Aphrodite,
and without *her* no pleasure left at all.

Exit Messenger.

44

CHORUS LEADER

I hesitate to speak the truth to you, the king,
but speak I will:
there is no god greater than Dionysus.

PENTHEUS

This Bacchic violence stands like a blaze at our doors.
We are shamed before Greece, and must move quickly. 780

He turns to a Servant.

You there! Go with speed to the Electran Gate
and muster the army: spearsmen, cavalry, archers.
We march against the Bacchae!
We will not be treated this way by women.
It is against nature!

Exit Servant.

DIONYSUS

You either didn't hear my words of warning, Pentheus,
or you ignored them. You have wronged me,
but I'm giving you another chance,
and so I'll warn you once again:
do not take arms against a god.
Stay here, at peace.   790
Bromius will not stand by
and let you drive his women from holy Cithaeron.

PENTHEUS

    I'll hear no lectures from you, an escaped prisoner.
    Unless you want to go back inside?

DIONYSUS

    If I were you I'd offer up a sacrifice, not a spear.
    You are a mortal against a god.

PENTHEUS

    Your god will get the sacrifice he deserves:
    the blood of his women, coursing down Cithaeron!

DIONYSUS

    You will be turned and put to flight, disgraced.
    Their fennel wands will pierce your shields of bronze.

PENTHEUS

    This man is impossible.   800
    Chains can't hold him, and he won't hold his tongue.

DIONYSUS

    Friend, you can still save the situation.

PENTHEUS

    How? By taking orders from my own slaves?

DIONYSUS

    No. I shall bring the women here.
    Back to Thebes and no blood spilt.

46

PENTHEUS

This is a trap.

DIONYSUS

A trap? How is that, when I'm saving you by my art?

PENTHEUS

You've made a pact with those women
to install forever this damn religion.

DIONYSUS

I made a pact, you're right, but with the god.

PENTHEUS

Servants, bring my armour from the palace.   810
And you: stop talking!

DIONYSUS

Ah . . . Wait . . . let me ask you: would you be interested in . . .
in spying on the women as they go about their mysteries?

PENTHEUS

I would give much gold for such a sight.

DIONYSUS

Such strong desire!

PENTHEUS

It would pain me, of course, to see them drunk.

DIONYSUS

But you'd like to see what gives you pain?

PENTHEUS

Yes, if I could watch them privately, discreetly;
under the fir trees, perhaps?

DIONYSUS

But if you try to hide, they might hunt you down.

PENTHEUS

Yes, you're right. I'll go openly.

DIONYSUS

Shall I take you there now? Will you try it?

PENTHEUS

The sooner the better. It would be a pity to waste time. 820

DIONYSUS

Very well. First you must put on a linen dress.

PENTHEUS

A *what*? You'd have me demoted to a woman?

DIONYSUS

If you show yourself as a man they'll kill you straight away.

PENTHEUS

Of course they will! You're very cunning.

DIONYSUS

Dionysus taught me everything I know.

PENTHEUS

So how do we do this?

DIONYSUS

We will go inside and I'll help you dress.

PENTHEUS

Please stop calling it a *dress*. I feel ashamed.

DIONYSUS

Are you not keen to see the Maenads?

PENTHEUS

What do I wear?

DIONYSUS

On your head, a wig of flowing hair.   830

PENTHEUS

And then?

DIONYSUS

A dress that stretches down to your feet,
and on your head a *head*-dress.

PENTHEUS

And after that?

DIONYSUS

A dappled fawn-skin and a thyrsus for your hand.

PENTHEUS

I can't bear it. All these women's clothes –

DIONYSUS

If not, you must fight the women and spill blood.
Either that, or watch them and spill –

PENTHEUS

Fine. I will be a spy in their camp.

DIONYSUS

That's wiser than pitting one evil against another.

PENTHEUS

And how shall I pass through Thebes without being seen?

DIONYSUS

We'll go by the back-streets. I'll lead the way.   840

PENTHEUS

Any way you want,
as long as those Bacchae don't jeer at me.

DIONYSUS

Let's go into the palace and get you ready.

PENTHEUS

Just give me a moment or two, to think this through.

DIONYSUS

Take all the time you like. I'm at your disposal.

PENTHEUS

Very well.
Either I go to the mountain dressed in armour,
or I take your advice.

Exit Pentheus into the palace.

DIONYSUS

He swims very fast, women, into my net.
He shall get to see the Bacchae
and the ticket will be death.

You are near, as always, Dionysus,
and now is the time for punishment.   850
First, drive him from his senses.
While he is sane he will never wear a woman's dress.

But he will shortly, as he is nearly mad.
After all those threats,
I want him walking down these streets in a frock;
I want him a laughing-stock.
Now I shall dress him for Hades,
where he will go by his mother's hand.
And he shall finally know Dionysus, son of Zeus,
a god both terrible and gentle to the world of man.   860

Exit Dionysus into the palace.

CHORUS
    Shall I dance them again, the nightlong dances?
    Dance again with bare feet in the dew?
    Shall I toss my head and skip through the open fields
    as a fawn slipped free of the hunt and the hunters,   870
    leaping their nets, out-running their hounds?
    She runs like a gale runs over the plain
    near the river, each bound
    and plunge like a gust of joy, taking her
    dancing, deep through the forest
    where no one can find her, and the dark
    is free and its heart is the darkest green.

    What is wisdom?
    The greatest gift of the gods is honour:
    to reach your hand in triumph up   880
    over the heads of the enemy.
    Honour is everything.

The might of heaven moves slowly, inexorably,
crushing men of arrogance
who disregard the gods.
The gods have time on their hands
in this long hunt for the unholy ones.   890
The old beliefs are simple,
and it costs nothing to believe.
Laws that have been built and changed
and strengthened through the ages
have become a true tradition, true to nature.

What is wisdom?
The greatest gift of the gods is honour:
to reach your hand in triumph up   900
over the heads of the enemy.
Honour is everything.

Lucky is the man who escapes a storm at sea
and finds his way home to safe harbour –
the man delivered from hardship.
We all compete for wealth and power,
and for every thousand hearts a thousand hopes.
Some wither, some bear fruit.
But the one who lives from day to day,   910
finding good where he can:
he is happy –
he is a lucky man.

Enter Dionysus.

DIONYSUS

Hello? Are you ready to go –
and see what you should not?
To desire what shouldn't be desired?
Come out, Pentheus, let's have a look at you.
Let's see you all dressed up in women's clothes,
disguised as a Maenad
and ready to spy on your mother
and on all those other women!

Enter Pentheus, dressed as a woman and carrying a thyrsus.

Now you *do* look like a daughter of Cadmus!

PENTHEUS

I see two suns in the sky;
two cities of Thebes, each with seven gates.
And you, my guide, you seem to be a bull.   920
Horns grow from your head.
Were you a beast all along? For you are a bull now.

DIONYSUS

The god is with us.
There were difficulties, but now we have a truce.
You see now what you should have seen before. The god.

PENTHEUS

So how do I *look*?
A little like Aunt Ino, or a bit more like my mother?

DIONYSUS

The very image of your mother, now I can see you plain.
But let me fix this curl that's come astray.

PENTHEUS

It must have been all that Bacchic ecstasy there in the palace.
I was shaking my head so much!   930

DIONYSUS

Then let me be your hairdresser. Hold still . . .

PENTHEUS

You arrange everything. I'm in your hands.

Dionysus adjusts Pentheus's hair.

DIONYSUS

Now your girdle is loose,
and the pleats of your dress are hanging crooked.

PENTHEUS (*checking over his shoulder*)
You're right about this side.
But the hem on the left falls perfectly to the ankle.

DIONYSUS

You will think me the best of friends
when you see what you don't expect:
Bacchae, chaste and pure.   940

PENTHEUS

    Would I look more like a true and proper Bacchante
    if I held the wand in *this* hand . . . or *this*?

DIONYSUS

    Use the right. Raise it up as you raise your right foot . . .
    This is an impressive change of heart.

PENTHEUS

    Could I lift up Cithaeron, do you think?
    Up on my shoulders, Bacchae and all?

DIONYSUS

    If you feel like it.
    You weren't of sound mind before, but now . . .
    Now you are as you should be.

PENTHEUS

    Should we bring crowbars,
    or shall I just put my shoulder to the mountain   950
    and pull it out with my bare hands?

DIONYSUS

    Steady now.
    You wouldn't want to damage the groves of the Nymphs,
    would you? Or the haunts of Pan where he plays his pipes?

PENTHEUS

    You're right, of course.

Brute strength is no way to master women.
I will hide in the firs.

DIONYSUS

You'll find all the security you deserve,
as a man who goes to spy on Maenads.

PENTHEUS

Just imagine!
I can see them already, deep in the undergrowth,
deep in each other, mating like birds . . .

DIONYSUS

That's certainly what you're planning to see.
You will catch them at it – unless you're caught first.   960

PENTHEUS

Lead me through the centre of Thebes.
I am the only one in this city brave enough to go:
the only true man in this whole city!

DIONYSUS

The only man to bear the city's burden.
Suffering lies ahead,
but you are worthy of such suffering.
So, follow me, I shall lead you safely there.
Someone else will bring you back.

PENTHEUS

Yes, my mother!

DIONYSUS

An example to everyone.

PENTHEUS

That is my goal.

DIONYSUS

You will be carried home . . .

PENTHEUS

What luxury!

DIONYSUS

. . . held in your mother's arms.

PENTHEUS

Ah, you spoil me.

DIONYSUS

Yes, you will be spoiled.

PENTHEUS

It's what I deserve!   970

Pentheus begins to leave the stage.

DIONYSUS

You are a fearsome young man,
and fearsome are the sufferings to which you are headed.
Your story will reach the towers of heaven.
Stretch out your hands to receive him, Agave!
And you, her sisters, daughters of Cadmus.
I bring this young man to a great defeat.
We already know he's lost,
and we have won: Bromius and I.
The rest will be revealed.

Exit Dionysus, following Pentheus.

CHORUS

Run to the mountains, swift hounds of madness!
Find the revels of the daughters of Cadmus
and rouse them in frenzy
against the man in woman's clothes,   980
spying on the Maenads!
His mother will spot him first, and call to her sisters:
'Who is this who has come to our mountain
to stare at us, my Bacchae?
Who gave birth to him?
He is not sprung from a woman's blood,
but is born of a lioness, or a Libyan Gorgon.'   990

Let Justice move forward, clearly,
let it move with sword in hand,

piercing the throat
of that godless, lawless, unjust man,
the earth-born son of Echion!

He walks towards your rites, Bacchus,
and those of your mother.
He walks against you,
with madness, rage and blasphemy,
thinking to control, by force, the uncontrollable.   1000
He walks, headlong, to death.
Acceptance, humility, moderation
all mean a life without grief;
but these are words he cannot even spell.
To live under the eye of the gods
we must give the gods their due,
be pure and pious if we want to live in peace.
To find happiness we must bow our heads,
as we stand under the aspect of heaven.   1010

Let Justice move forward, clearly,
let it move with sword in hand,
piercing the throat
of that godless, lawless, unjust man,
the earth-born son of Echion!

Come to us now, Dionysus, come to us as a bull!
As a many-headed serpent, as a lion in flames!
Come with the grin of a beast, Bacchus,
and throw out the net of death!

The man who hunts the holy Bacchantes   1020
is now their running prey.

Enter Second Messenger.

SECOND MESSENGER
These halls were once so prosperous, so happy,
that they were famous throughout Greece.
The house of Cadmus of Sidon
who sowed the dragon's teeth and harvested men!
I mourn this house, and its falling.

CHORUS LEADER
What's happened? What news of the Bacchae?

SECOND MESSENGER
This is the news. Pentheus, son of Echion, is dead.   1030

CHORUS LEADER
All hail to Bromius! What a god you are!

SECOND MESSENGER
What? You rejoice, woman, in the death of my king?

CHORUS LEADER
I am no Greek, and he was not my king.
I praise my lord in my own way.
This news frees us from the fear of chains.

SECOND MESSENGER

There are still men in this city
who can wield the power of law.

CHORUS LEADER

It is Dionysus, not Thebes, who has power over me.

SECOND MESSENGER

I understand your allegiances, woman,
but there's no need to glory in our grief.   1040

CHORUS LEADER

We'll see, once you tell me the final act.
How did the tyrant die?

SECOND MESSENGER

Three of us went. I was attending Pentheus,
and the stranger was acting as our guide.
We'd left behind the last farms
on the outskirts of Thebes,
crossed the river Asopus
and reached the rocky uplands of Mount Cithaeron.

We stopped in this grassy glade:
silent and vigilant, like scouts,
seeing without being seen.
There was a deep glen, with steep sides down   1050

to the stream that flowed through it,
where dense pines grew and gave some shade
to the Maenads sitting there.
Some were busy, winding fresh ivy round
their tattered fennel wands; some – frisking
like fillies that had slipped their painted bridles –
were singing Bacchic songs, one to the other.

Unhappy Pentheus, though, could not quite see
the women well enough.
'Stranger,' he said, 'from where I stand,
I can't make out their Bacchic frenzy. Perhaps   1060
if I climbed that huge fir that overhangs the banks
I could get a better view of their wanton orgies?'

And then the stranger worked a miracle.
He reached for the highest branch of the great fir and,
slowly, pulled it down,
down, down to the black earth
till it was curved taut as a bow,
tight as the circle of a wheel.
He did what no mortal could do:
he drew this mountain fir
down to the ground till its tip was at his feet.
He sat Pentheus there at the top of the tree   1070
then let the trunk pass through his hands, slow,
slow, slow, so as not to throw the wobbling king,

till it rose and straightened up to heaven
with my master balanced at the top.
Then he saw the Maenads.
But not as well as they saw him.
And at that moment,
the stranger was nowhere to be found.
And from the sky came a great voice –
Dionysus, it must have been – crying out:
'Women, I bring you the man who mocked me,
denied my sacred mysteries,   1080
the man who mocks you now.
Take him for his crimes!'
And as he spoke,
an arc of lightning
crackled between earth and heaven.

The high air hushed, the leaves sat still;
even the birds and beasts fell silent.
The Bacchae stood, ears pricked, glancing around.
They had heard the voice but not the words,
and so he spoke again.
And this time they knew him.
The daughters of Cadmus, and all the Bacchae,
knew the command of the god.
They broke with the blankness of doves –   1090
flying through the glen and over its rocks and rapids,
maddened with the hot breath of the god.

Once they saw him again, my master in his tree,
they climbed a bluff opposite his perch
and started pelting him with stones,
throwing fir branches over
like javelins, their fennel wands like spears.
But all fell short.
Poor Pentheus in his cage, unable to escape;   1100
just out of range, just out of reach.
Finally, they sheared limbs off an oak
and tried to lever the fir up by its roots.
But that failed too. So Agave shouted:
'Come, my Maenads,
gather round this tree and all take hold.
We must shake loose this climbing beast,
for he will reveal the secrets of the god.'
And with that, countless hands pulled and pushed
and tore the fir tree out of the earth,   1110
and from his high roost Pentheus fell,
down, down, down, crashing head first
through the branches to the ground,
screaming now as he understood his fate.

His own mother,
like a priestess with her sacrifice, fell on him first.
But he snatched off his head-dress and wig
so she could see who he was.
He reached out his hand to touch her cheek
and cried out: 'Mother! Mother! Look!

It's me, Pentheus, your own son!
The son you bore to Echion!   1120
Spare me, Mother, I beg you!
I have done wrong, perhaps,
but you cannot kill your son!'
But Agave's eyes were rolling,
and her mouth filling with foam.
In the grip of the god and the god's frenzy,
it was as if she couldn't see him, couldn't hear.
Grabbing his left hand at the wrist,
she planted her foot against his flank and wrenched,
pulling his arm straight out of his shoulder –
not with her own strength but the strength of the god.
Ino worked on the other side,
tearing off handfuls of skin,
while Autonoe and all the other Bacchae came, engulfing
    him.   1130
The air was full of yelps and cries
and he heard what must have been his last scream,
delivered to this world with his last breath.
A shriek of triumph. One woman cradled an arm;
another had a foot still warm in its shoe.
His ribs were clawed down to the white,
and every woman's hands were daubed with blood
as they tossed chunks of him
back and forth like a game of ball.

His remains lay scattered:
some under the jagged rocks,
some lost under the leaves of the deep forest.
Agave found his hopeless head, I know that much.   1140
She pushed it onto the end of her fennel wand
and carried it high through the glades of Cithaeron.
She seemed to think it was the head of a mountain lion.
Leaving her sisters to their dances,
she has reached the city walls.
I heard her calling out to Bacchus,
her 'fellow huntsman', her 'companion
in the chase', in the 'taking of the prize'.
The only prize that she takes home is grief.
I cannot bear to stay and see Agave in the palace;
I have seen enough disaster for one day.
This is another lesson:
that moderation and reverence for the gods   1150
are a mortal's best possession.

Exit Second Messenger.

CHORUS
Let us dance for the glory of Bacchus!
Let us dance for the death of Pentheus –
offspring of the dragon
who dressed as a woman
and carried a thyrsus,
and was led to his death by a bull!

EURIPIDES

Let us hail the Bacchae of Thebes!   1160
A victory song, then a slow lament!
To hold your beloved only son,
in arms drenched with his blood!

*Enter Agave, carrying a thyrsus, with the head of Pentheus
impaled upon it.*

CHORUS LEADER
Look! It's her! Pentheus's mother, Agave,
hurrying wild-eyed to the palace.
Let us welcome her
to the happy company of the blissful god!

AGAVE
Bacchae of Asia . . .

CHORUS
Tell us.

AGAVE
. . . I bring this sprig, newly cut, from the mountain.   1170
The hunting was good.

CHORUS
We see you and welcome you, fellow reveller.

AGAVE

I caught it without traps or snares.
It's a young cub, a mountain lion, as you can see.

CHORUS

Where did you catch him?

AGAVE

Cithaeron . . .

CHORUS

Cithaeron?

AGAVE

. . . brought him death.

CHORUS

Who killed him?

AGAVE

The honour of the first blow fell to me.
The Maenads call me 'blessèd Agave'.   1180

CHORUS

Who else took part?

AGAVE

Cadmus's . . .

CHORUS

Cadmus's?

AGAVE

. . . daughters. They reached him after me.
But I was first.
The hunting was good.

CHORUS

An impressive catch, blessèd Agave.

AGAVE

Then share in the feast.

CHORUS

Share what, you poor woman?

AGAVE

The cub is young and tender.
Feel the down on his cheek. How soft his hair is.

CHORUS

Yes, his wild hair makes him look like a beast.

AGAVE

Our god is a wise god. A hunter.   1190
Dionysus whipped us on against this thing. We Maenads.

CHORUS

Yes, our king is a hunter.

AGAVE

Have I done well?

CHORUS

You've done well.

AGAVE

Soon the men of Thebes . . .

CHORUS

And Pentheus, your son . . .

AGAVE

. . . will praise the mother who caught this whelp
and brought him home.

CHORUS

An extraordinary catch.

AGAVE

Extraordinary skill.

CHORUS

Are you happy?

AGAVE

    I feel the thrill of having done something great
    with this plunder, something plain to see!

CHORUS

    So, poor woman, show the citizens what you caught,   1200
    this trophy you have brought back from the hunt.

AGAVE

    Look at this, men of Thebes,
    citizens of this towered city,
    look at the prize!
    The beast brought down by the daughters of Cadmus –
    not with nets or spears
    but the pale and delicate hands of women.
    You armed hunters should look,
    think hard, and then stay silent,
    because we caught our prey and tore it to pieces
    with nothing but these hands, these white blades.
    But where is my father, Cadmus?   1210
    He should be here.
    And where is my boy, Pentheus?
    Have him bring a ladder;
    that beam up there is a perfect place for a hunting trophy.
    For the head of this young lion I have killed.

Enter Cadmus with Servant carrying a draped stretcher.

CADMUS

Follow me, please,
and bear the dreadful burden in before the palace
and set it down.
The pieces that were Pentheus.
How long I searched for him – all
dismembered through Cithaeron's glens and woods,
no two pieces in the same place – and now   1220
I've assembled him, this gory jigsaw, as best I could.

Old Tiresias and I had already left the mountain
and were back in Thebes
when I heard the news
of my daughters' terrible deeds.
I retraced my steps to Cithaeron
to bring back this boy the Maenads had slaughtered.
There in the forest I found Ino
and Autonoe – who bore Actaeon to Aristaeus, and so
had seen it all before –
but both were still stricken with the madness.
Agave, I was told,
was on her way to Thebes, still possessed.   1230
And they were right, for here she is.
It is not a happy sight.

AGAVE

Father, you have the right to make the proudest boast,

for you have sired the bravest daughters in the world.
And of us all, I am the foremost:
leaving the shuttle and loom for bigger things –
hunting animals with my bare hands.
As you can see, I have a trophy for our house,
to hang here on the wall.

She holds out Pentheus's head.

Here, Father, take it in your hands.   1240
Share the glory of my kill
and invite your friends to a feast of triumph.
You are blessed, blessed by my accomplishment.

CADMUS

This is a grief beyond measure.
Pentheus was rightly named, for sorrow.
You and your sisters call yourselves hunters,
but this is murder. This is butchery.
You say this broken king is a sacrifice to the gods,
that we should call a feast of praise,
inviting Thebes, inviting me?
I pity you for your grief to come, and I pity myself.
We must have deserved the justice of Bromius,
our own god, but he has been so just, so terribly just,   1250
he has destroyed us all.

AGAVE

Old age turns men so miserable.

74

I wish my son took after me,
going out on the chase
with his young friends from Thebes.
But all he does is quarrel with the gods.
You must have a word with him, Father.
Where is he, anyway?
Someone call him here
so he can witness his mother's good fortune.

CADMUS

Enough.
If you ever realise the dreadful things you've done,
it will drive you mad.   1260
Better you stay demented as you are,
as that might save you.

AGAVE

Where is the shame? Where is the cause for grief?

CADMUS

First turn your eyes to the heavens.

AGAVE (*looking up*)
Well? What am I meant to be seeing?

CADMUS

Does it look the same as before? Or has it changed?

AGAVE

It's brighter. Clearer.

CADMUS

That thrilling inside you – do you still feel it?

AGAVE

Thrilling? I don't understand.
I . . . I feel . . . I feel something slowing down.   1270
Yes, I feel something in my head is clearing.

CADMUS

Can you hear me still? Can you answer sensibly?

AGAVE

I'm sorry, Father. I can't remember.
What were we talking about?

CADMUS

Into which house did you marry?

AGAVE

I married Echion. One of the Sown Men, they say.

CADMUS

And the name of the son you bore your husband?

AGAVE

Our son is Pentheus.

CADMUS

And whose head do you hold in your hands?

AGAVE (*averting her eyes*)

A lion's . . . The huntresses . . . They said . . .

CADMUS

Look at it properly. Just a quick glance.

AGAVE

What is it? What am I holding in my hands?   1280

CADMUS

Look closely now. Be sure.

AGAVE

Ah! No! No! I see the greatest sorrow.

CADMUS

Does it still look like a lion?

AGAVE

No! No. It is . . . Oh gods! It is Pentheus's head I hold.

CADMUS

Now you see who I was mourning.

AGAVE

Who killed him? How did he come to be in my hands?

CADMUS

This is too hard, this truth. It took so long to come to this.

AGAVE

Tell me! Please! My heart beats with terror.

CADMUS

You killed him. You and your sisters.

AGAVE

Where did it happen? Here, at home? Where? 1290

CADMUS

On Cithaeron, where the dogs tore Actaeon apart.

AGAVE

Cithaeron? But why was Pentheus *there*?

CADMUS

He went to mock the gods, and your rituals.

AGAVE

But *we* – why were *we* there?

CADMUS

You were out of your wits.
The whole city was possessed by Bacchus.

AGAVE

I see. Dionysus has destroyed us all.

CADMUS

You enraged him. You denied him as a god.

AGAVE

And where, Father, is the rest of my poor son?

CADMUS (*pointing to the stretcher*)
Here. I found all I could.

AGAVE

Is he complete, and decently arranged?   1300

[. . .]*

But why should Pentheus suffer for my crime?

CADMUS

Like you, he refused the god.
And so the god ruined us all:
you, your sisters, and this boy.
This house is destroyed as well, and me with it.
I have no male heirs, and now I have lived to see

---

* A lacuna in the original text. Agave may have joined her son's head to the rest of his body.

the fruit of your womb so shamefully destroyed.
(*addressing the corpse*) It was through you, my boy,
that this house regained its sight.
It was you, my daughter's son,
who held the palace together and the citizens in line.   1310
It was you who protected me from insults in my old age –
and you who would punish anyone who slighted me.
But now I shall be dishonoured,
an outcast from my own home.
I, Cadmus the great, who sowed the Theban race
and reaped that glorious harvest.
Dearest of men – for even in death
I count you as the man I love the best –
no more will you stroke my beard, child,
no more will you hug me, call me 'Grandfather' or say: 1320
'Has anyone wronged you or shown you disrespect?
Has anyone disturbed or hurt you?
Tell me, Grandfather, and I will punish them.'
But now there is grief for me and a shroud for you,
and pity for your mother and her sisters.
If anyone still disputes the power of heaven,
let them look at this boy's death
and they will see that the gods live.

CHORUS LEADER
    I am sorry, Cadmus,
    but your grandson has had the justice he deserves,
    however hard it is for you.

AGAVE

Father, you see how changed my fortunes are . . .

[. . .]*

Dionysus appears now revealed as a god.

DIONYSUS

. . . you, Cadmus, will be turned into a snake,   1330
as will your wife, Harmonia, daughter of Ares.
Then both of you, according to the oracle of Zeus,
will be drawn by oxen in a cart,
lead a barbarian horde and sack many cities.
When your army plunders the shrine of Apollo, though,
its homecoming will be dangerous and unhappy.
But Ares will save you both,
and bring you to the Land of the Blessed.   1340

I, Dionysus, speak these words.
I, no son of a mortal, but of Zeus.
If you had shown sense before,
you would have found happiness, and an ally in me,
the son of Zeus.

---

* A further lacuna. The first section was perhaps a lament by Agave over her son's body; the second the beginning of Dionysus's speech.

CADMUS

Dionysus, we ask for mercy. We have done wrong.

DIONYSUS

Too late to know me now.
You did not know me when you had the chance.

CADMUS

We have learned. But your punishment is harsh.

DIONYSUS

I am a god! You treated me with contempt.

CADMUS

Should gods not stand above all mortal passions,
such as anger?

DIONYSUS

Long ago my father Zeus ordained that this would
come to pass.

AGAVE

Father, our banishment is decreed.   1350

DIONYSUS

Then why delay all this?
All this which, I have said, must be?

Exit Dionysus.

CADMUS

What a terrible end we have come to, my child –
you, your wretched sisters and me.
An old man,
I must go and live as a stranger among barbarians.
Not only that; the oracle says
I must lead an army against Greece.
But worst of all, Harmonia and I
must sack the tombs and shrines of Greece –
both of us transformed into serpents!   1360
There will be no end to my suffering.
Even as I cross the river Acheron as it plunges down,
still I will have no peace.

AGAVE

But I, Father, must go into exile without you!

She embraces him.

CADMUS

Poor child, why put your white arms around me?
A swan sheltering an old weak man in her plumage.

AGAVE

Where shall I go, banished from my country?

CADMUS

I do not know, child.
Your father is no help to you now.

AGAVE

Farewell, my home!
Farewell, my city, farewell my marriage bed!
Driven from you, I leave you in despair.   1370

CADMUS

Go, my daughter, to the house of Aristaeus.

AGAVE

I grieve for you, Father.

CADMUS

And I for you, dear daughter, and your poor sisters.

AGAVE

Terrible is the ruin
Lord Dionysus has visited on this house.

CADMUS

Terrible the treatment he received from us:
his name was dishonoured in Thebes.

AGAVE

Farewell, Father.

CADMUS

And farewell to you, unhappy child.
Though how you will fare well is hard to see.   1380

AGAVE

Take me, guides, away from here,
to my sisters: sisters of my endless exile.
Let me go where vile Cithaeron cannot see me –
where I can never see Cithaeron, or another fennel wand!
All of that I leave behind, for other Bacchae.

Exit Agave and Cadmus, in different directions.

CHORUS LEADER

The gods take many shapes,
accomplish many things beyond our expectations.
What we look for does not come to pass;   1390
what we least expect is fashioned by the gods.
And that is what has happened here today.

Exit Chorus.

GLOSSARY

ACHELOUS (ak-uh-**loh**-uhss, ak-i-**loh**-uhss), a river in western Greece.

ACTAEON (ak-**tee**-uhn, **ak**-ti-uhn), son of Aristaeus and Autonoe, grandson of Cadmus, he was a hunter who chanced upon the goddess Artemis bathing; as a punishment she turned him into a stag and he was devoured by his own hounds.

AGAVE (uh-**gah**-vay, uh-**gah**-way), daughter of Cadmus, mother of Pentheus.

AGENOR (uh-**gay**-nor, a-**gay**-nor), father of Cadmus.

APHRODITE (af-ruh-**dy**-ti), daughter of Zeus, the goddess of love and beauty.

APOLLO (uh-**pol**-oh), son of Zeus and Leto, the god of prophecy, music, medicine and poetry, sometimes identified with the sun.

ARES (**air**-eez), god of war, son of Zeus and Hera.

ARISTAEUS (arr-i-**stee**-uhss), husband of Autonoe, a daughter of Cadmus.

ARTEMIS (**art**-im-iss), daughter of Zeus and Leto, the virgin goddess of the hunt and the twin sister of Apollo.

ASOPUS (a-**soh**-puhss), a river of Boeotia originating on Mt Cithaeron.

AUTONOE (aw-**ton**-oh-e, aw-**ton**-oh-i), a daughter of Cadmus.

AXIOS (**ak**-si-oss, **ak**-si-uhss), a major river that rises in Macedonia, also known as the Vardar.

BACCHAE (**bak**-y, **bak**-ee), the female followers, attendants or priestesses of Dionysus/Bacchus.

BACCHUS (**bak**-uhss), the counterpart of Dionysus in the Roman pantheon.

BACTRIA (**bak**-tri-uh), country lying between the mountains of the Hindu Kush and the Amu Darya in what is now part of Afghanistan, Uzbekistan and Tajikistan.

BROMIUS (**brom**-i-uhss), name for Dionysus ('the thunderer' or 'he of the loud shout').

CADMUS (**kad**-muhss), founder of Thebes, son of the Phoenician king Agenor.

CITHAERON (ki-**thy**-ruhn, ki-**thy**-rohn), a mountain range between Boeotia in the north and Attica in the south, it was sacred to Dionysus, and the scene of many notable events in Greek mythology: Oedipus began and ended his life here – abandoned by his parents to die on its slopes as a child and then wandering there blind as an old man; Actaeon was torn apart there by his own dogs, and it is where Heracles hunted and killed the Lion of Cithaeron.

CORYCIA (korr-**iss**-i-uh), the ridges of Corycia are on Mt Parnassus, the site of the Corycian Caves.

CURETES (koo-**ree**-teez), the nine dancers who praise Rhea, the Cretan counterpart of Cybele, with drumming and dancing.

CYBELE (**sib**-il-i, **sib**-uhl-i), the mother of the gods, originally Phrygian, the goddess of nature and fertility.

DELPHI (**del**-fi, **del**-fy), an ancient town of central Greece near Mt Parnassus, and the site of a famous oracle of Apollo.

DEMETER (duh-**mee**-tuhr, dim-**ee**-tuhr), goddess of the harvest and fertility.

DIONYSUS (dy-uh-**ny**-suhss), son of Zeus by Semele, cousin of Pentheus and Actaeon, god of vegetation and fruitfulness, known especially as the god of wine and ecstasy.

DIRCE (**deer**-kay), Boeotian river with its source in the west of Thebes. Outside the city it joined the Ismenus.

DITHYRAMBUS (dith-i-**ram**-buhss), name for Dionysus used at his festivals, referring to his double birth.

ECHION (**ek**-i-ohn, **ek**-i-on), husband of Agave and father of Pentheus; one of the surviving 'Spartoi' that sprang up from the dragon's teeth sown by Cadmus.

ELECTRAN GATE, one of the seven gates of Thebes.

ERYTHRAE (**err**-ith-ry), a municipality in Boeotia.

EVIUS (**e**-vi-uhss, **e**-wi-uhss), a name for Dionysus.

EVOHÉ (ev-**oh**-ay), a call of praise to Dionysus.

FATES, the Moirai, who controlled the metaphorical thread of life of every mortal: Clotho, who spun the thread; Lachesis, who measured it out; and Atropos, who cut it.

GIANTS, the Gigantes ('the earth-born'), huge monstrous men, were closely related to the gods.

GORGON (**gor**-guhn), a monstrous female creature whose appearance would turn anyone who laid eyes upon it to stone.

HADES (**hay**-deez), the underworld, named after its god.

HARMONIA (har-**mon**-i-uh), the wife of Cadmus, goddess of harmony and concord.

HERA (**heer**-uh), the queen of the gods and the consort of Zeus, goddess of women, marriage and childbirth.

HYSIAE (**hiss**-i-y), a city in Boeotia.

IACCHUS (i-**ak**-kuhss), a name for Dionysus.

INO (**y**-noh, **ee**-noh), daughter of Cadmus, wife of Athamas.

ISMENUS (iss-**men**-uhss, iss-**mee**-nuhss), Boeotian river with its source in the east of Thebes. Outside the city it joined the Dirce.

LYDIA (**lid**-i-uh), an Iron Age kingdom of western Asia Minor.

LYDIAS (**lid**-i-ass), river in Macedonia.

MAENAD (**mee**-nad, **my**-nad), a female follower, attendant or priestess of Dionysus.

MEDES (meedz), people of the Median Empire in Iran, one of the four major powers of the ancient Near East along with Babylonia, Lydia and Egypt.

NYMPHS, female spirits of the natural world.

NYSA (**ny**-suh), the mountainous district where Dionysus was raised by the rain-nymphs, the Hyades. Its location is unknown and variously associated with Ethiopia, Libya, India or Arabia.

OLYMPUS (uh-**lim**-puhss), Mount Olympus in Pieria, northern Greece, the home of the gods.

ORPHEUS (**or**-fi-uhss, **or**-fyooss), a legendary Thracian poet and musician whose music had the power to move even inanimate objects and who almost succeeded in rescuing his wife Eurydice from Hades.

PAN, god of shepherds and flocks.

PAPHOS (**paf**-oss), a coastal city in the south-west of Cyprus.

PENTHEUS (**pen**-thi-uhss, **pen**-thyooss), king of Thebes, grandson of Cadmus, son of Echion and Agave, cousin of Dionysus.

PHRYGIA (**frij**-i-uh), a kingdom in the west central part of Anatolia, in what is now modern-day Turkey, where Dionysus learnt the mysteries from the goddess Cybele or Rhea.

PIERIA (py-**eer**-i-uh), in the southern part of Macedonia, Pieria is the home of Orpheus and the Muses, as well as the Pierian Spring.

RHEA (**ree**-uh), daughter of Uranus and Gaia, she was known as 'the mother of gods' and was associated with Gaia and Cybele.

SARDIS (**sar**-diss), now known as Sart, in Turkey, it was the capital of the ancient kingdom of Lydia.

SEMELE (**sem**-uh-li, **sem**-i-li), daughter of Cadmus, she was seduced by Zeus and was the mortal mother of Dionysus.

SIDON (**sy**-duhn), a city in Phoenicia, now the third-largest city in the Lebanon. Founded by Agenor, father of Cadmus.

THEBES (theebz), a Boeotian city-state, situated to the north of Mt Cithaeron.

TIRESIAS (ty-**ree**-si-uhss, ty-**ree**-si-ass), the famed prophet of Thebes who was transformed by Hera into a woman for seven years, and blinded by Athena, and who features in *Oedipus Rex* and the *Odyssey*.

TMOLUS (**tmoh**-luhss), a mountain in Lydia.

ZEUS (zyooss, zooss), the principal god of the Greek pantheon, ruler of the heavens, and father of other gods and mortal heroes.

THE HISTORY OF VINTAGE

The famous American publisher Alfred A. Knopf (1892–1984) founded Vintage Books in the United States in 1954 as a paperback home for the authors published by his company. Vintage was launched in the United Kingdom in 1990 and works independently from the American imprint although both are part of the international publishing group, Random House.

Vintage in the United Kingdom was initially created to publish paperback editions of books bought by the prestigious literary hardback imprints in the Random House Group such as Jonathan Cape, Chatto & Windus, Hutchinson and later William Heinemann, Secker & Warburg and The Harvill Press. There are many Booker and Nobel Prize-winning authors on the Vintage list and the imprint publishes a huge variety of fiction and non-fiction. Over the years Vintage has expanded and the list now includes both great authors of the past – who are published under the Vintage Classics imprint – as well as many of the most influential authors of the present.

For a full list of the books Vintage publishes,
please visit our website
www.vintage-books.co.uk

For book details and other information about the classic authors we publish, please visit the Vintage Classics website
www.vintage-classics.info

www.vintage-classics.info